WORKPLACE ETIQUETTE

WORKPLACE ETIQUETTE

How to Create a Civil Workplace

Includes Business Meeting & Business Meal Etiquette

By Rebecca Black

CELESTIAL ARC PUBLISHING

Third Edition: Entirely revised in 2019 with additional material.

CELESTIAL ARC PUBLISHING

ISBN-10: 1545424985
ISBN-13: 978-1545424988

DEDICATION

To my dearest friend and loving husband Walker Black. You have been my most ardent supporter and the very best editor a writer can have.

CONTENTS

INTRODUCTION

"There is no accomplishment so easy to acquire as politeness, and none so profitable." George Bernard Shaw

Whether working in a grocery store, government office or for a Fortune Five Hundred Company, one should follow a particular code of conduct. Civilized decorum, best known as etiquette, is expected. Albeit, some feel that proper etiquette is stuffy and outdated. This view is far from true.

Etiquette is basically the behavior that is expected when in a public shared space. A workplace is no different from any other shared space. It is much more pleasant when everyone behaves in a polite and respectful manner.

All sharing the workplace would benefit greatly by creating the kind of working environment that each would want to work in. To do this, each of us must use our basic manners, no matter what our level in the organization. Through our behavior, all of us can make a difference. We can create a working environment free from the typical stress-inducing negativity.

THE IMPORTANCE OF BUSINESS MEETING ETIQUETTE

It is common for today's businessperson to spend about one quarter of their working time in meetings. Worse yet, a CEO may spend much more time. This fact emphasizes the need for effective, civilized business meetings. However, where should we begin?

Remembering our basic manners and office etiquette while planning and participating in the business meeting is a great place to start. The number one rule? Don't have a meeting if you don't need one!

CONSIDER THESE QUESTIONS

Why do people dislike meetings? It could be because many times we feel as if meetings are just one big waste of our time.

Why do we engage in business meetings? The meeting is thought of as the best way to disseminate information. It brings people together for a common purpose. It can motivate the workforce as a team and promote group thinking. It also creates ideas that may not have been applied to an objective.

What do we all need to do in order to have a successful meeting? In addition, what, as participants, should we do in order to demonstrate interest at our business meetings? These questions plus much more will be answered in the Business Meeting Etiquette chapter.

WHY BUSINESS MEAL ETIQUETTE?

Many job candidates face a meal interview. Additionally, it is quite common for most to experience business meals from time to time. During these working breakfasts, power lunches, and all other business meals, all manners are scrutinized. Therefore, we need to be prepared.

Throughout this book, the author comprehensively covers the previous topics and much, much more. You, the reader, will learn how to create the type of workplace in which you'd would want to work.

Enjoy!

CHAPTER ONE
ETIQUETTE IN THE WORKPLACE

RESPECT & KINDNESS

"Do not be concerned about others not appreciating you. Be concerned with you not appreciating others." Confucius

Displaying kind and respectful behavior helps create the kind of working environment in which we would want to work. Thus, our starting point is the basics. As simple as it may appear on the surface, basic manners like saying please, thank you and you're welcome help build and retain relationships. These words – and the meaning behind them – are the building blocks of all our manners.

We tend to trust those who know to use these basic words of manners. Without them, we could not cultivate those working relationships we need to be successful. Additionally, the workplace would – most likely – be sterile and unpleasant. After all, we spend a disproportionate amount of time at work.

It is common knowledge that we spend up to 85% of our lives at work, thinking about work, or driving to and from work. That is an enormous part of our lives. Moreover, because work is a *huge* part of our lives we should smile more.

Yes, again I'm mentioning a very small, simple act. A smile may seem simple and irrelevant, but it is powerful. For example, have you noticed that when you smile most people smile in return? Smiling, especially when accompanied by good eye contact, is another excellent trust-building tool to help build our working relationships. Considering the cost of motivational seminars, the simple smile is extremely cost effective.

THE EFFECT OF A POSITIVE ATTITUDE IN THE WORKPLACE

Many moons ago I worked for a male boss in a public school with four female coworkers. It was a miserable situation. My boss didn't respect women one iota. He called us *his* girls and belittled us in front of others.

One morning I woke up in the very best mood, a mood too good to lose. Therefore, I made a conscious decision to take that mood to work with me. I consciously decided that there was no way I would *allow* my boss's attitude to ruin my day.

I arrived to work early as usual, opened the school with the custodian and prepared for the day. My boss arrived soon after. Here I was sporting this great mood, smiling, asking how his evening was, and generally enjoying the morning. It was amazing to witness the change in that typically acerbic man. Uncharacteristically, he was polite and helpful. My workmates arrived a bit later and asked me if I had drugged him. Of course, I told them I hadn't. I was just nice. I had to wonder if I was partly responsible for his negative moods. I'll never know.

Every day we need to choose our attitudes, because our attitude is how others view us. So, enjoy the day and smile. The best managers are those who know to smile and greet people every day. Perhaps that grouchy person who never smiles or says hello will too.

THE POWER OF COURTESY

If we truly want to create the type of environment in which we want to work, consider that courtesy is a powerful tool as well. Not everyone is compatible and some people tend to clash, but we can and should circumvent negative feelings with courtesy. Simply consider how you would like to be treated, and then act accordingly.

Creating a positive atmosphere in the workplace is everyone's job.

Knowing that not everyone is compatible, we must strive for positive interaction between coworkers and those you serve. Consider this; your coworkers can help or sabotage you so subtly you may never see it coming. If you talk down to those around you, your work will suffer and of course, the opposite is true. If you are kind and considerate, others will treat you similarly.

For example, let's take a common work situation. Imagine that you work in a unit with a boss – Nancy – and a couple of office assistants who often assist you in completing your reports. They do not work for you; they work for the unit. One day, your boss, Nancy, assigns a task and would like it finished before you leave. You finish the assignment, but would like the formatting altered. Thus, you walk over to one of the assistants, plop it down on his desk and say, "Nancy would like this done by 5."

The assistant looks at the document and replies, "Gee, it looks important, but I just don't have the time." Does the assistant have time? Don't know. Were you rude to him? Well, not in the *strictest* definition of the word. Nevertheless, you *disrespected* him. You talked down to him as if he is lower than you, which, by the way, no one is lower than anyone else.

Follow along for how this scene *should* have played out. You receive your task, do your part, and walk over to the office assistant, Bob. You say, "Bob, I can see that you have a lot of work on your desk and I hate to have to ask you this, but do you think that you have time to do this for me, please?" More than likely Bob will say yes. Why? There are three reasons.

Reason number one, you remembered to say his name. Everyone has one and we all like to hear it. Two, you recognized that Bob contributes; he is an important member of the unit. We all want recognition. Finally, you said, "please." Even schoolchildren realize that this is a magic word; it works wonders.

Perhaps all of this appears simple and a bit silly to consider that just by behaving more civilly you can make a difference in the workplace. Nevertheless, consider the multitude of books and plethora of articles written each week in many major business publications dictating everything suggested here. Business and career-development writers appear to say the same simple, silly things: be nice and treat others with respect.

One of my favorite books on the subject is <u>The Power of NICE</u>, by Linda Kaplan Thaler and Robin Koval. Please read it. It is enlightening.

HOMEWORK

Use your perception skills and notice how you treat those with whom you work. Then, improve your workplace relationships using everything mentioned in this chapter.

TIME TO USE THE MATERIAL

1) Why is etiquette in the workplace important?

   _____

   _____

2) Why is projecting a positive attitude important in the workplace?

   _____

CHAPTER TWO
PERSONAL INTERACTION

EFFECTIVE COMMUNICATION

Tell me and I will forget. Show me and I'll remember. Involve me and I'll understand. *Chinese Proverb*

Communication is fundamental in all relationships, with *listening* as the most important component. It is essential to listen attentively to our co-workers and our customers. When we listen attentively, we are validating the speaker; and we all want to feel validated.

Listening attentively or the act of "being there" helps us to create the type of workplace in which we all want to work. It is *essential* to "be there," to be in the moment and focused when others are speaking. When we are not listening, we don't respond appropriately and the speaker becomes frustrated. Thus, our behavior creates a negative response.

Additionally, speaking clearly, avoiding slang and euphemisms is most preferable, as more than likely, a few of your coworkers or customers do not speak English well. To say, "Two peas in a pod" or "That website is cool" may be meaningless and confusing to many.

MORALE DESTROYING BEHAVIORS

Creating a negative working environment is actually quite easy. Follow along as I mention a couple of moral destroying behaviors to avoid.

Avoid using condescending tones. None of us appreciates others speaking down to us, as if we were little children. This behavior is boorish and causes talent to rush for the doors.

Anyone could become impatient at one time or another when someone requires repeated instruction. However, using condescending tones with those who are in training or in need of extra help is counterintuitive. It also speaks very negatively about us.

So, try to empathize, as not everyone understands the first time around—or perhaps the third. Patience and understanding is key, it demonstrates respect for that person and the position you hold.

Using vulgarities in the workplace is another minefield. For example, a very good friend of mine retired early because she could not take one more day of her manager's vulgar language, condescending tones and moodiness. Not one person in the office respected her and morale was nonexistent. No one should be subjected to this infantile behavior.

Bravo for you if you are living in the perfect world where everyone with whom you work follows this advice. Unfortunately, however, all too often this is not the case.

Constructive Feedback vs. Blaming

Constructive feedback is an important component of communication in the workplace. Some do not always respond well to constructive feedback, as they may feel as if it is a personal attack.

Personally, as a writer I need constant feedback. I need editors who are ruthless with the red pen. Through the assistance of my red-pen wielders, I have become a better writer than I was *just* last year. Moreover, I am positive that I will be a better writer next year, because of that very effective communication tool, constructive feedback.

That is exactly what constructive feedback is *supposed* to be--an effective tool to help all of us to be the best at *whatever* we wish to be. Nevertheless, we must use it correctly. We must never accuse, blame, or attack when we are in the position to dole out feedback.

It helps to remember that each in the workplace is a member of a team. All work together. If someone was to makes a mistake, everyone should take some responsibility in it. Perhaps that person needed assistance. Perhaps the task needs to be altered for it to be accomplished correctly.

Case in point. Most often, when I ask attendees of my business etiquette workshops how they approach a coworker with a *perceived* mistake, I receive the same story. Many reply that as they discuss the issue with the mistake-making coworker, they find that he/she was taught to perform the task in that manner. Thus, there was no mistake; there was just more than one protocol for the same task. Now with the real problem exposed, the two coworkers could work toward a solution.

Alternately, if the coworker had approached the mistake-making coworker with a negative, blaming tone, she would have shut down. We tend to shut down when others approach us using negative tones. Never play the blame game; it is counter-productive and hurtful.

If we make a mistake, we must own up to it quickly and attempt to find a correct method for performing the task. Avoiding informing others of our mistake would be irresponsible.

SHOWING RECOGNITION

Showing recognition for a special favor, interview, or opportunity to present our ideas is essential for building relationships. I believe all of us want to know that our efforts matter.

When we use those little words, "thank you," we are recognizing the hard work of those around us. It really is magic.

Thank you notes are also quite effective, especially when sent in a timely manner. For example, a representative from a local Senior Center approached me to present a speech for their members. Actually, I was surprised and honored, as they usually ask doctors! So of course, I replied in the positive before they could realize their mistake.

I presented my speech, thoroughly enjoying myself. It was pure joy to have had the opportunity to do so. Everyone, including staff, was very grateful, verbalizing their thanks after my speech. Thus, I honestly wasn't expecting anything more from them. However, the very next day, I received not just a thank you note, but a thank you *letter*—very impressive. Will I ever do anything for the Senior Center again? You bet.

This is the power of recognition.

HOMEWORK

Improve your listening skills by "being there" while others are talking. Also, write a thank you note to someone who has performed a special task.

TIME TO USE THE MATERIAL

1) What is the most important component of communication?

   _____

   _____

2) Why is constructive feedback so important?

   _____

   _____

   _____

CHAPTER THREE

HONESTY & INTEGRITY

WHAT IS HONESTY ANYWAY?

"Honesty pays, but it doesn't seem to pay enough to suit some people." F.M. Hubbard

Honesty is imperative in the workplace; in fact, it is imperative in everything we do. I believe that most everyone wants to be honest and feels as if they are. However, some appear to have a quirky disconnect considering what a dishonest act is.

Case in point, I recently conversed with the owner of a local coffee shop. As I sipped, she lamented about her quest to find suitable employees. Her most recent hire thought it appropriate to make complimentary, special coffees for his friends. When she confronted him, the surprised young man stated that he wanted to *please* the customers. He had no concept that his actions were essentially stealing and meant lost sales for her.

During another interview, she shared that the candidate gleefully stated that he enjoyed his last job immensely, because he could drink coffee all day. When she queried about what his cost of the coffee was, he stated, "Why should I pay, they are a large corporation; it doesn't cost them anything." Hmm.

People run and own companies—*people*. When employees take things, even a paper clip, it is stealing...stealing from people. When job candidates lie about their past, they lie to people. When a coworker takes credit for another's idea, he/she is dishonest to a *person*.

The principles we live by every day and in every situation is what defines us as human beings. In all situations, including the workplace, we should all remember our values.

"Where is there dignity unless there is honesty?" Marcus Tullius Cicero

HOMEWORK

Take note! Are you as honest in the workplace as you feel you should be? Improve if not.

Time To Use The Material

1) What percentage of what we see do we remember?

   Fill in the blanks:

   Honesty is _____ in the _____; in fact, it is imperative in

   _____ we do.

CHAPTER FOUR
APPEARANCES

APPEARANCES MATTER

"We don't live in a world of reality, we live in a world of perceptions." Gerald J. Simmons

Appearances can affect working relationships and relationships with customers. Imagine how customers view these disconcerting workplace etiquette faux pas: engaging in personal conversations and eating at one's desk while customers are waiting. Besides the fact that these behaviors are unprofessional, the focus is not customer centric. In both instances, the customer could feel unimportant.

The desk is also no place for grooming. The best place to touch up makeup, floss teeth, clean fingernails, brush hair and shave is the restroom. To perform these activities at your desk suggest that you are not interested in your work and that you have no manners.

Some years ago, I had a colleague who flossed her teeth every day after lunch. Flossing after eating is an excellent habit to possess; however flossing at the lunch table is not at all appealing. Just the two of us lunched every day in our classroom. I suppose she considered her actions appropriate because I was the only other person in the room. *That* is a big no. Please consider everyone as important as your most important client.

SELF-CONFIDENCE AND SELF-IMAGE

Body language is vitally important in everything we do. Just imagine the person who stoops with head down. He appears to be self-conscious and unengaged. However, someone who stands tall, head up, and walks confidently, is taken seriously and appears self-confident. It is all about perception.

Once upon a not-too-long-time-ago, a college professor asked three groups of his students to pretend. Each group was to pretend either to be popular, to be unpopular, or to be the average Joe/Jane.

At the end of a predetermined amount of time, 85% of those who pretended to be popular were, those who pretended to be unpopular were, and those who pretended to be the average Joes/Janes were.

What is this exercise illustrating? People believe what they see. Moreover, we believe the response we receive from others. We tend to become the person others perceive us as, because actions precede feelings. For example, if we assume the actions of a confident person, others respond as if we are that confident person, we then believe it. In fact, a number of social scientists now concur.

Thus, if we wish to be viewed and treated as a confident professional, we need to behave as such.

Finally, always remember that you have less than a minute to make a good impression. Therefore, besides body language, our attire and behavior is essential as well. Every aspect of dress and behavior adds or detracts from the business environment.

Hygiene

Always ask yourself what impression others have about me.

Have you had to sit next to someone or work next to someone who had questionable hygiene? Not the most pleasant situation, is it? Proper hygiene is imperative.

Consider what one city had to do because of one employee. City officials, state that one smelly employee is responsible for a new policy that requires all city employees to smell nice when at work.

"No employee shall have an odor generally offensive to others when reporting to work. An offensive body odor may result from a lack of good hygiene, from an excessive application of a fragrant aftershave or cologne or from other cause."

This may be an extreme reaction to a poor hygiene issue. Nevertheless, it is a great example of how our society feels about body odor. Consequently, bathe every day. Brush your teeth, wash your hair, and pay close attention to the cleanliness of your clothing. Glance at your nails. They should be clean and well groomed.

One problem men tend to experience as they age is unexpected hair appearances. One day your ears are smooth, the next there is this strange growth. Scrutinize nose and ear hair. Yes, this is not the most pleasant subject, but necessary. Gentlemen care for their appearance. Moreover, they never do so in public, such as cleaning ears or nose in the company of others.

We have our own issues, ladies. One day, while in a grocery store I noticed a well-dressed woman wearing a very nice pair of slacks and a sweater set tending the courtesy clerks. From her attire and demeanor, I assumed she was their manager. Unfortunately, she decided that it was a bit too warm and took off her outer sweater. I say unfortunately because the professional, lady-like image of her magically erased from my mind. She had not shaved and was wearing a sleeveless sweater. Ladies attend to their grooming. Moreover, they never do so in public, such as cleaning ears or nose in the company of others.

ATTIRE BASICS

Visualize the Erin Brockovich character from the movie of the same name. No one took her seriously, although she was quite brilliant. Why? Her attire did not reflect a business aptitude.

Albeit we all have our personal style, most times it is best to leave it at home for the sake of the position we hold. With a keen eye toward our attire, it is doubtful that we would experience the prejudices Erin did.

Speaking of attire, consider how you dress for work. Do you have a clear idea of what is appropriate and what is not? For many it is not so clear. Look around you. If you are wearing jeans and a t-shirt to work while others are wearing dress shirts, ties and slacks, then perhaps you should amend your clothes closet. Dress in a similar style as your co-workers or aim a bit higher and *dress for success*—comparable to your supervisor.

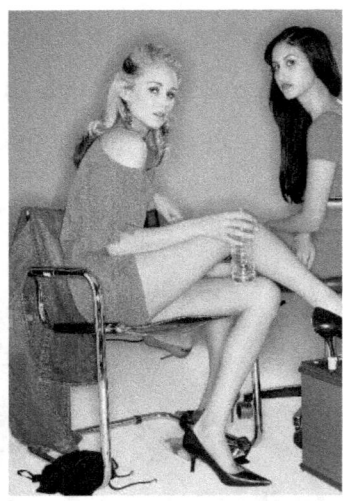

Perfect attire for a modeling job, but not so for most positions.

Unfortunately, women need to be especially cautious about work attire. This subject is a veritable minefield, but it is one that must be broached. *We cannot allow our bodies to do the talking for us.* The message may not be what we had intended. By this, I mean that skintight shirts (micro-fiber) and short skirts, or perhaps the low-waist skirt and shorter top that allow for a view of skin may give others the impression that we care more about showing off our perfect waistlines than job performance. It is not professional.

Also, consider casual Fridays and its impact on professional appearance. Many people wear jeans and casual shirts on Fridays and it may not be a negative. However, every day is a good day to make a good impression. For instance, you never know when your big chance will come or if that major client will appear. So casual Fridays may still be a great idea, albeit with some caveats.

Consider what business casual should be. For men in the workplace this means collared shirts – always tucked in – slacks, and polished shoes with laces. Blouses tucked in, appropriate-length skirts or slacks, and comfortable shoes that are neither sneakers nor flip-flops is a great look for women.

When in doubt, ask clothing store personnel or emulate your boss's choice in attire.

Finally, we all need to be team players. Reflecting upon Erin again, she antagonized those around her. Remember, that you are not alone at work; you interact constantly, so always think about the comfort level of those around you. This is the essence of respect and kindness.

CLOTHING CHOICES MAKE AN IMPRESSION

I was just talking to a new friend and she shared a story from her childhood. As a teen, she was just beginning a new math class in high school. The first day of school, the teacher walked in looking rather scruffy wearing jeans and a t-shirt. The students were unruly, noisy, and not much work was accomplished that day.

The very next day, the teacher walked in wearing a suit, hair groomed, and using excellent posture. Everyone sat up in their seats, quieted down, and showed the teacher proper respect. His only words: "Don't ever think that proper attire is not important." "People will judge you by the way you are dressed." She says that is the best lesson she ever learned and she will never forget it.

QUALITY IS NOTICED

Studies support the fact that observers trust and believe those who *appear* more successful, educated and capable. Color is a substantial part of that.

Colors and different shades of the same color affect people's impression of the wearer. Color announces your status, effectiveness, attitude, loyalty, honesty, and credibility.

Inexpensive clothing from discount stores does not dye the same as higher quality clothing. The colors are harsher than and not as rich as in higher quality clothing. Observers view this as shabby and second rate.

My favorite method for learning the difference in quality clothing is to window shop. Go to the highest and lowest quality-clothing store to touch, feel, and take notes.   I find that taking pictures helps also. Compare all your notes. Soon you will be able to recognize quality by the color and feel.

Additionally, you will soon realize that you don't have to spend a lot on clothes to look like you've spent a lot once you can tell the difference in color and feel. Nobody sees the label

See Colour Affects http://www.colour-affects.co.uk/research

BUSINESS DRESS CODES

CORPORATE

This dress code applies to law firms, investment banking, and any company that is considered conservative. Men wear suits, with shirts (usually white), and ties. It's best for women to wear a suit as close to male colleagues as possible, blouse or crisp shirt, stockings, and closed-toe shoe with a low to medium heel.

BUSINESS APPROPRIATE

This dress code applies to everyone who wants to make a good impression. It is a polished look that includes jackets with high-quality dress shirts and slacks and maybe a tie for men. Women could wear a skirt with a blouse or sweater set. Another excellent choice would be tailored trousers paired with a turtleneck and jacket.

BUSINESS CASUAL

Business casual is not sloppy attire; it is pressed and immaculate. For men, this look continues to be conservative with slacks such as Dockers, shirts with buttons, sweaters, and shoes that require polishing. It is best to have a jacket nearby just in case for both genders. For women, it is much the same, except that a simple dress or skirt with a refined top would work also.

Please do not wear tank tops, printed t-shirts, anything too short, too tight, too sheer, or too low-cut

HOMEWORK

Use all the information you learned in this chapter to improve your workplace wardrobe and appearance. Show off the best of who you are!

TIME TO USE THE MATERIAL

1) Why is body language so important in the workplace?

_____

_____

2) Why is attire choice so important?

_____

_____

3) Studies support the fact that observers trust and believe those who *appear* more successful, educated and capable. What is one of those elements that helps us "appear" more successful?

_____

4) What is the basic definition of "Corporate Attire"?

_____

_____

_____

CHAPTER FIVE

DISABILITY ETIQUETTE

How to Begin?

Consider how you would like to be treated if you had a disability. Most likely, you answered, "Just like everyone else." Those over sixty are becoming a majority and our roadways are crowded and dangerous, which means more and more people are at risk for devastating illnesses or accidents. So that person in the wheelchair could be any of us—a disturbing thought, I know.

Although the ADA provides literature dictating legal responsibilities of business owners, ignorance of special needs is still pervasive. Wheelchair ramps and accessible bathrooms are a good beginning, but many of us are not aware of the devices required by the disabled or the handicapped. This is especially problematic for business owners and those in supervisory positions, since they are responsible for providing the tools to assist everyone to reach their potential.

Add to this complexity of the issue that there are many types of disabilities, some more visible than others. Thus, you may need to be diligent in your search to assist.

Tools for Working With the Disabled

When addressing those with disabilities, please do not use condescending language as if the person is a simpleton. A disability does not equate to a lack of intelligence.

For Those Who are Deaf

Do not shout at the deaf, it is not constructive or polite. Simply get the person's attention and speak clearly, as he may be trying to read your lips. Notes help; email and texting are great tools as well.

For Those Who are Blind

Isn't it amazing that some will also yell at the blind or sight impaired as if that will help the person see what that person is gesturing toward? This is silly and not necessary. More than likely he hears just fine; however, make sure he is aware that you are talking to him.

If he appears disoriented, offer your arm without grabbing him. Imagine being in a dark room, unable to see anything and someone grabs you. Always consider how you would feel in a similar situation.

For Those With Speech Impediments

For those who have speech impediments, please do not finish their sentences. Listen patiently and repeat anything unclear. Usually, the more comfortable the person becomes with you, the clearer his speech becomes.

For Those in Wheelchairs

Returning to the subject of wheelchairs, here are a few things to consider. Do not pat a person on the head as you would a pet. When talking to those in wheelchairs, sit in a chair if possible to establish eye contact. Those in wheelchairs are in a disadvantage, as they need to look up when talking to others causing neck strain.

In addition, never lean on the wheelchair while conversing. The chair is more than just transportation; it is a lifeline to the world. It is also his personal space.

Recently I was taught a very important lesson in acceptance. I was bound to a wheelchair for a short period and had trouble getting through a heavy restroom door. A woman rushed up behind me insisting upon helping. After politely refusing her assistance, she replied, "Now don't be so proud and let me help you." Consequently, I did.

I realized that I needed the help and she *needed* to provide it. Her positive attitude made a permanent impression on me. I will always accept help when it is needed.

Just imagine that you witnessed a person with a bag of groceries walking in front of you. The bag ripped causing apples to roll everywhere. Would you help that person? Of course, you would. Your first instinct would be to rush over and start gathering and talking to the poor apple-losing soul.

So if you witness a person with a disability struggling, offer to help. Be specific; say something like, "Please allow me to open the door for you." If the person is insulted or refuses, don't take it personally. We can only offer; this is the essence of respect and kindness.

Courtesy is a gift we give freely with no thanks required.

HOMEWORK

Get to know the disability policy in place for your workplace.

TIME TO USE THE MATERIAL

1) What are the tools for working with the deaf?

   _____

   _____

2) What behavior is best when talking to a person in a wheelchair?

   _____

   _____

CHAPTER SIX
DIFFICULT SITUATIONS

DEALING WITH DIFFICULT PEOPLE

Handling difficult people like those obnoxious people who pull in front of you on the freeway and that person who tries to sneak in front of you when you've been standing in line for an hour can be a challenge. However, in the workplace, you need razor sharp coping skills.

Most often, it's mutually beneficial to seek a polite way to manage a conflict. For example, imagine a woman coming into an office seeking assistance. With her are two small children. She does nothing to prevent them from tossing items from near-by desks or stepping on other customer's feet. What to do?

For this common occurrence, you have two problems to solve with the children as your first priority. There is a safety issue along with the irritation of your other customers. One method of response could be to inform the mother that you want to assist her, but due to your concern for the safety of her children, it may be best that she asks the children to sit down. Then it is possible to listen attentively to her problem.

Alternately, you could provide the children with an activity to distract them, like color crayons and paper or puzzles.

Another common issue is the *very* angry, loud, difficult-to-please customers. What to do? Angry people want to vent. Allow the person to vent as long as he is not violent or abusive--no one is expected to accept that kind of behavior. Listen while looking at the person and withhold your opinion. Repeat your understanding of the problem and discuss a solution.

Sometimes there is no solution. However, state how you would like to help and ask for his or her suggestions.

Notes

Angry Customers?

Place yourself in his shoes. Step back, lower your voice and speak softly, repeating what you believe the problem is. Then, seek help if you can't solve the issue.

Never say that it isn't your job.

Angry Boss?

Either leave or speak up, never responding with emotion. Schedule a time to speak in private and discuss his/her behavior and how it disturbs productivity, while documenting everything.

Praise him/her when the behavior changes. However, if the behavior doesn't improve, seek assistance from HR or his/her superior (if there is one).

Multiple Difficult Situations?

Remind yourself that the situation may be difficult now, but not later. If it is a challenge, seek out those who have dealt with similar situations—online is fine. There are many resources available these days. You have the choice of how to handle the situation, unless there is policy in place.

Try to be positive and remember that you don't live with the situation.

When in the presence of others, take your emotions out of the issue—then let loose in private.

In private, laugh, keep a journal, discuss the issues with those you trust, and engage in nurturing activities you enjoy.

HOMEWORK

Consider how you would handle all these difficult situations. Write your ideas down and then revisit your document in a month. Do you still agree with your first ideas? Did you think of other methods?

TIME TO USE THE MATERIAL

1) How do we deal with angry customers?

_____

_____

_____

_____

CHAPTER SEVEN
CULTURAL AWARENESS

INTRODUCTION

Many Americans believe that they have no culture, but this is far from true. What is true is that Americans come from many countries with diverse cultures. So how is it possible for this mass of people from all parts of the world to have a culture and a unique etiquette? We try harder.

No, I am not trying to be cute here. Actually, Americans try very hard to achieve more—more of everything, such as money, and success. We genuinely believe that we can and will make a difference, that the underdog can win, and that if we try hard we can do it all. In fact, Americans are a bit arrogant about our individualism and freedom to explore any interest.

For a person from another country to arrive today, to study, work, or live, it may be a bit daunting to try to fit in. Personally, I see the difficulties some young people experience because I live in a university town.

Therefore, to celebrate our differences and to prepare those of you from another country trying to fit in, we will explore America's unique culture as it relates to etiquette.

AMERICANS ARE...

President Ronald Reagan once stated that his favorite letter he received while in office was from a foreigner living in the United States. *Paraphrasing* from the letter, the man wrote "...the United States is the only country in the world that once you live in it, you can become a part of it. If you move to France, you are never a Frenchman. If you move to Germany, you are never a German. But, when you move here, anyone can become an American."

Therefore, while it is true that many of us are from another country, together we make up the *'us'* the *'we'* the *Americans*. Moreover, we bring with us our rich traditions and cultures. Some may seem a bit strange to another of a different ethnicity. Still, no matter where we were born or what cultural influences we follow, *we* would choose to be happy over success, wealth or power. This is just one commonality we share.

America is an excellent place to live because we have an enriching cultural and ethnic diversity. We have a rich blending of peoples and traditions. Getting to know these traditions and learning that we are more a *part of them* than *apart from* them should be our ultimate goal.

Because we are a people of diversity and inclusion, we open our arms to all. Because of this, we will encounter those from other countries or cultures who do not value things as we do. This is very important for all of us to be aware of, but of special note for those who work closely with the customer.

For example, Americans value personal space at about one arm's length. Many cultures do not. *Who is wrong here?* Are we wrong when we back up when someone enters our personal space? *No.* We need to honor everyone's difference and be aware that everyone is different.

Collect those cultural differences or traditions and make those that you admire your own. We are a people of many cultures and traditions, mutts if you will. Moreover, we all know that mutts are the healthiest. Right?

For myself, I have *collected* the Asian tradition of removing my shoes before entering someone's home. In my opinion, it symbolizes respect for the person and his home.

Note

My International Business Travel Etiquette Book may be of interest: http://www.amazon.com/International-Business-Travel-Etiquette-Understanding/dp/1500125229/ref=pd_rhf_dp_p_tnr_2

HOMEWORK

What cultural tradition would you like to keep for yourself?

ETIQUETTE OF THE AMERICAN PEOPLE

RESPECT

As Aristotle stated many years ago, *"People are virtuous because they act rightly."* This means that we do the right thing and then we become the virtuous person.

Hence, when we use proper manners such as, opening doors for people, saying good morning to neighbors, and just being kind, soon we are that 'kind' – or virtuous – person without thinking. It becomes a part of us. Those around us become nicer, kinder and more considerate as a result of our example—something we should consider in the workplace as well.

In our culture, respecting others is very important and the absence of it is noticed. Nevertheless, respect begins with us. Bathing and grooming is essential.

In many parts of the world, bathing every day is thought of as unnecessary and downright silly. Not so here. Americans are sensitive about body odors.

Smiling is also significant. It is appropriate and welcomed to smile at most everyone you may see on the street. Of course, there are exceptions. New York City dwellers are notorious for not making eye contact and being a bit standoffish or in your face (ish). However, for the purpose of this book and this subject, I am referring to the *majority* of Americans. Moreover, the majority of us smile.

Americans smile with their entire face exposing their teeth.

In one of his many travel books, Rick Steves – a respected travel writer – stated that the French view those walking around smiling as simpletons. Other cultures may hold the same view. Therefore, for some from another country, smiling may be difficult to become accustomed. However, a smile goes a long way here. We tend to gravitate toward and trust the person who smiles and withhold our trust from those who do not.

Family is also very important, but we have a few unique differences here. Because Americans tend to move around quite often, our family structure may not compare to those in other countries; however, we compensate. We endeavor to spend time with them. Although, sharing meals is often a burger in the car on the way to a soccer game. Additionally, staying in touch with out of town family – even parents – may be by email or video call.

There are countless studies as regards to how parents can do a better job, which is an indication about how important "family" is to most Americans.

SHARED SPACES

"Shared Space" is the term I use to describe places the public shares, like the workplace, stores, restaurants, etc. Most significantly, we use a special etiquette in these shared spaces. For example, dressing appropriately for special events, job interviews and even for the workplace is paramount.

Americans tend to be laid-back, casual people, but most realize that our clothes represent how we wish to be perceived, as evidenced by the plethora of articles and books written about the subject recently.

Public transportation is a shared space.

When dressing for the ballet or some other special event please avoid shorts, jeans, sandals, and tennis shoes, even though you may see others wear them. Even many Americans simply do not know that they should dress more formally, which is unfortunate.

Specific attire is also essential for a job interview. Your attire choice will have an effect on the interviewer--positive or negative. So in most situations, avoid short skirts, bright, flowery prints, open shirts and baggy pants that hang down past the hips. When you acquire a job, dress for success. If you project a positive image through clothes and stance, others will notice it too.

Use good judgment in shared spaces. Look around, get a feel for what others are wearing and doing. Be aware of your space, including tone and volume of your voice. Smoking is frowned upon these days, so do not smoke near another and do not overindulge in alcohol. No one wants to be around a tipsy, sloppy, nicotine soaked person.

In addition, although cellphone use in public is common and widespread, most consider it ill-mannered to talk loudly while in the company of others. Using a cellphone in a restaurant – and many other shared spaces – is considered rude and many restaurants are now creating policies to ban its use.

Speaking of restaurants, endeavor to be on time for reservations. Time is very important and tardiness is considered rude.

Use all your manners: please, thank you, excuse me and of course, table manners. Treat the wait staff with respect. Now, you don't have to become chatty with them, but saying "thank you" is expected.

If someone is paying for your meal, please remember to thank the host. If not, keep in mind that tips are not generally included in the checks in the United States.

Note

- Gentlemen remove their hats inside buildings, especially in restaurants.

ELEVATOR ETIQUETTE

Surprisingly, we use a specific etiquette for elevator use. Actually, there is a special etiquette for most everything we do. Why would elevator riding be any different? Therefore, when riding an elevator, we should take our manners with us.

There's not much etiquette involved when the elevator is crowded, as the person closest to the door exits first. There is no gender consideration; the first consideration is expediency. However, when the elevator is not crowded women and girls enter and leave first unless there are elderly aboard. If so, they trump everyone else. Our elders are considered special and important, so we part the way and allow them to enter and exit first.

Until everyone is either on or off, the person closest to the 'Door Open' button should hold it. Imagine if an elevator door closed on someone and we could have prevented it—not nice.

HOLD THE DOOR

If you approach a door before someone else, open it for that person, no matter who he or she is. Usually, you will find a surprised smile and you may have helped to propagate good manners in others.

Common sense tells us that we should hold the door for a person carrying packages. That person cannot possibly open the door for herself.

A mother with a stroller needs assistance as well. Most likely, she will be very happy to receive a little extra help. Equally, we should extend this simple gesture for anyone needing assistance, such as someone in a wheelchair.

Men should hold the door for women. Men and boys should always behave as gentlemen and as ladies we should allow them to do so.

It's best to hold the door for anyone close behind us. Can you imagine a door slamming shut in your face because you were following someone and he had forgotten to hold the door for you?

HOMEWORK

What manners/behaviors do you notice in shared spaces?

COMMUNICATION

Americans consider communication vital. However, there is some unique etiquette to observe, such as the time of day that it is appropriate to call someone. When using the telephone/cellphone, identify yourself to the caller and do not call others before 9 am or after 9 pm.

Communication is best when accomplished face to face. In some cultures, to look in one's eyes as they talk is not proper. Here it is essential. We consider it polite to make eye contact with those who are speaking. The same is true when we speak to others. For Americans, it is a trust issue. Thus, if someone looks at us while he is talking, he appears to be trustworthy.

It is also considered impolite to interrupt others while they are speaking.

Besides eye contact, which is imperative, a strong handshake is necessary when being introduced. A firm, not too firm, grip with a dry right hand is best. Try not to shake the person's arm out of its socket, just a gentle up and down motion will do.

RULES OF INTRODUCTIONS

Introduce younger people *to* their elders: Additionally, introduce guests to hosts.

As a sign of respect, introduce people *to* others with higher standings such as senator, governor, mayor, clergy, etc.

In business, introduce the less senior person *to* the more senior associate.

HOW TO INTRODUCE OTHERS

Always introduce people by their first and last name, preceded by their title and followed by a bit of information specifically about them. For example, "Good morning, Professor Jane Frank, I would like to introduce *to* you, my colleague from work, who shares your enthusiasm for rare books, Mr. Pedro Garcia. And Pedro, this is my neighbor who owns the wonderful collection I was telling you about."

It is not necessary to repeat names. As you notice above, I mentioned Professor Jane Frank only once. This proper for social situations. In my introduction, I included information about each person and possibly instigated a new friendship.

Now, let's take a look at introducing a younger person to the elder and the less prominent person to the more prominent. If Pedro had been elderly and Jane much younger, I would have introduced Jane to Pedro. Moreover, if Pedro had been a clergy member and Jane a writer, I would have introduced Jane to Pedro. *Always* follow this rule in business.

Now as you have probably noticed, I refer to Professor Jane Frank as Jane, and Mr. Pedro Garcia as Pedro. This is because these are my fictional friends designed to help illustrate proper introductions. I would never introduce anyone, including fictional friends by only their first names. In fact, there are specific instances that I would never include a first name in an introduction, such as a boss, client, or someone more prominent than I.

A proper greeting would be to say, "It is so nice to meet you." It is always best to repeat that person's name, because not only it is polite, but also because doing so will help you remember the name. This is especially helpful in business.

ELECTRONIC COMMUNICATION

Just follow good old fashioned, proper behavior and you can't go wrong." Charlotte Ford

I believe a good portion of the world uses similar electronic etiquette. However, what follows is the expected behavior here in the U.S.

Use email wisely. It *is* a form of writing so use your best letter writing skills, and watch the vulgarities. Do not constantly forward pages of jokes; it takes too much time and is rarely appreciated, especially in the workplace. Additionally, it is entirely acceptable to use email for sending birthday cards and letters. The focus is that you remember people.

EMAIL & INTERNET USE AT WORK

Recently, it cost a large integrated oil and gas company $2.2 million in a lawsuit for an offensive email. An employee sent this email, "25 reasons why beer is better than Women" to coworkers. He sent it as a joke not realizing the consequence. Degradation in the workplace is a huge no-no.

Note

- More information is available in Chapter Nine.

CELLPHONE ETIQUETTE

Universally, it would seem, our cellphone has become a part of our everyday life. Sometimes it seems is as if we are born with one stuck in our hands, as if we can't get through the day unless we have them on and readily available for that ever-important call.

I believe most of us have the-rude-cellphone-person story to tell, like the one I just heard from a close friend. Evidently, a stylish and a bit preoccupied woman who frequents one of our more up-scale hair salons uses her cellphone during her time in the chair. Okay, that might not seem as such terrible behavior, granted. Nevertheless, it gets worse.

Her cell was on "speaker phone" for all to hear. While her hair was soaking in the latest dye job, she chatted away...loudly. She had no idea – or cared for that matter – that others really don't want to share her cellphone conversation. Let's try to remember that everything we do affects other people, which includes our cellphone use.

Note

Please don't take pictures of others without permission.

Do

- Use an earpiece in high-traffic or noisy locations.
- Remove Blue Tooth device when with others.

No Ringing

- In a restaurant, library, place of worship, court or hospital.
- During a doctor/dental exam, discussion with another person, or an interview.
- In a theater during a movie or at the golf course.

Avoid Conversing

- In every situation mentioned above.
- While a checker in a store is ringing up your purchases.
- During a haircut or styling.

Avoid loud melodic ringing in public places

TEXT MESSAGING

Today, electronic communication is part of our lives. And, why not? It is fun, quick, and effective. Nevertheless, we need to observe some etiquette. We would not want to be rude to those with whom we communicate.

Do not text someone, while in the company of another.

- It is considered just as rude as taking a voice call.

Text messaging is informal.

- It should not be considered for formal invitations.

Do not dissolve a relationship using text messaging.

Be patient while waiting for a reply.

- Watch your frustration level; your recipient may not know how to use this service as well as you.

Be aware of your tone.

- Your message can be misinterpreted. Reread your messages carefully.

Texting while driving is a no-no.

- There is no possible way anyone can watch the road and text at the same time.

Watch your slang.

- Yes, this is an informal form of communication, but slang and poor grammar can become part of your everyday language.
- Stay on top of your game using proper language and grammar.

Texting can be traced.

- Do not transmit improper messages.

Absolute Social Networking No-No (s)

- Cyber dumping

- Sharing personal information

- Posting racy or potentially embarrassing photos

- Posting hateful or untruthful gossip about others

- Using profanities

- Using poor grammar

WRITTEN COMMUNICATION

It is quite common for Americans to communicate feelings with greeting cards. Write thank you cards when receiving a gift, after attending a party or dinner, and if someone performs a special favor for you. Cards are also sent for times of grief or celebration, such as a death or a wedding.

THANK YOU NOTE SAMPLE

Date

Dear Mr. Jones,

Your current projects sound very interesting and I believe that I could be a valued member of your team. Thank you for opportunity to present my ideas.

I look forward to our next meeting.

Sincerely,

Emily Jones

HOMEWORK

If from another country, list five differences in etiquette you notice from your culture compared to the U.S. Compare the differences carefully to help fully understand them.

These are the basic American principles of etiquette. Next, let's explore American culture.

AMERICAN CULTURE

HOW WOMEN ARE VIEWED

American's consider men and women equal, so they are treated in the same manner in business situations.

However, in social situations men are still expected to treat a woman as a lady. For example, men open doors for women and allow them to enter first. Additionally, in a restaurant, women are usually seated and asked about their orders first.

Found in management positions and positions of authority, women are treated with the same respect as her fellow male counterpart. In fact, during meetings and business meals women are considered part of the team. To behave in a condescending manner toward women is frowned upon.

PERSONAL FREEDOMS

Personal freedoms are crucial to us, such as *freedom of religion.* So expect a variety of places to worship. All freedoms are valued. For example, we don't always agree with ideas, beliefs, and comments that are guaranteed by our *freedom of speech*, but most Americans will fight for the right to express them.

INDIVIDUALISM

Individualism is highly regarded. We celebrate those who leave the comfort of the familiar to travel the unknown and at times frightening path. People like Marin Luther King Jr., champion of civil rights, Nelson Mandela, fighter against Apartheid, and Eileen Marie Collins, astronaut, pilot, and the first woman who in 1999 commanded a space shuttle are among our heroes.

TIME

Time is valuable as Americans pack more into a day than seems rational. We work a longer week than most and take fewer holidays. During a vacation, it is common for an American to schedule activities for each day, but leave little time for rest. Work, or a person's profession, somewhat defines that person; we take our jobs seriously.

Because time is so highly valued, when invited to someone's home, be on time. In some countries, like France for example, it is considered rude to arrive on time; one is expected to arrive about 20 minutes later than the stated time. However here, it is considered impolite and disrespectful to arrive late.

DISCUSSING WORK

It is common to be asked what you do for a living in social settings, such as dinners and parties. However, this is not a time to go on and on about a latest project or promotion; this kind of behavior is viewed as boorish. Just relax and join in the conversation.

HOMEWORK

What cultural difference are you having the most difficulties with and how will you adapt?

GESTURES

Americans smile with their entire face with teeth exposed.

Winking could be interpreted as a form of flirtation so it should be avoided—unless you are flirting.

Pointing a finger at anyone is rude, but pointing at something you want is proper.

Picking your nose or teeth in public is rude, as is chewing fingernails.

HAND GESTURES

Hand gestures mean different things to different cultures and ours is no different. Sticking your middle finger out from your fist will incite anger in others. Just as a thumb sticking out of your fist means everything is going on schedule, or is fine.

Most recognize the "Peace Sign" gesture to mean "Peace."

Come

Hand close to body and facing up, wagging your fingers in and out. Alternatively, do the same with just the index finger.

Crossed Fingers

This means the person is hoping for good luck.

Indicating an Interest in Something

Point with index finger. Never point at people.

Getting a Waiter's Attention

Make eye contact and slightly raise a hand.

OK

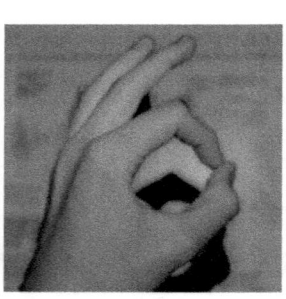 

A thumb raised out of closed fist. Alternately, it could be an open hand with index finger meeting a thumb.

Stop

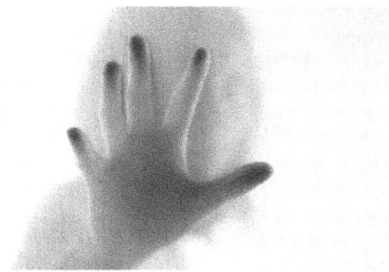

Hand up, palm facing forward with no movement, or hand waving front to back means no, stop, or go back.

Waving Hello or Good-By

Wave hand back and forth bending fingers forward or wave entire hand from side to side.

Yes and No

Shake head up and down for yes, and back and forth for no.

DIFFERENCES FOREIGNERS MAY ENCOUNTER

FORMS OF ADDRESS

The family name is second, such as Rebecca Black. Black is the family name. Mr. is used before a man's name, such as Mr. Walker Black. Mrs. is used before a married woman's name, such as Mrs. Rebecca Black.

Miss is not used much anymore for unmarried women, but you may hear it occasionally. Ms. is used commonly for married and unmarried women, for example: Ms. Rebecca Black.

Friends do not typically use titles when referring to each other.

ELECTRONIC EQUIPMENT

- 110-120 volts, 60 cycles, you may need an adapter

NUMBERS

- Dates are written as month/day/year..
- The number 13 is considered unlucky, so there is usually no 13th floor in buildings..
- The number 7 is considered lucky..
- A US trillion is 1 followed by 12 zeros, a British billion
- A US billion is 1 followed by 9 zeros, a British millard
- A period indicates a decimal point: 5.5

- A comma separates a group of numbers: 231,542,000

TABLE MANNERS

Americans use the crisscross method for their fork and knife. However, many are now using the continental method as well.

TIPPING

Only tip, or leave a gratuity, in restaurants that offer table service—typically not for fast food. However, if a coffee house has a "tip jar" on the counter, a small tip – usually 25 cents – is fine.

Most restaurants do not include a gratuity (tip) in the bill. You may ask if a gratuity is included in your bill. If not, (and it is usually not) add 15%-20% to the bill, depending on the service you received. Alternatively, place the gratuity on the table when you leave.

15% is a typical tip for taxi drivers and hair stylists.

If assisted with bags (valet or bellhop) or a car (valet, parking garage attendant) a dollar per bag/car is appropriate. Pay when your bag is delivered or the car is returned.

Please do not try to tip a police person, it is considered bribery and is illegal.

WEIGHTS

Americans use weights and measures, such as pounds and gallons.

WORDS FOR TOILETS

Toilet	Bathroom
Men's room	Women's room
Lavatory	Little boy's room
Potty	John
Restroom	Head

An outhouse is a toilet located outside. A porta potty is a toilet in a recreational vehicle or a public toilet at an outdoor event.

In the US, there are few public toilets; you may find some in gas stations, hotels, bars or other public places. Some public toilets use an automatic flush. Consequently, if you find no handle, it will flush automatically.

NOTES

- Individualism, freedoms and personal space are highly regarded.
- Time use defines Americans, as well as eye contact.
- Personal hygiene is important; bathe daily.
- When invited to dinner, arrive at stated time, take a hostess gift (wine, flowers, or candy--something similar) and send a thank you note.
- Business meetings are very important; arrive on time. Call if you expect to be late.
- Business meals are for business; food and socializing are not the focus.
- Women are often found in management and authoritative positions.
- A strong handshake is positive.
- Dress informally, except for interviews, work, special cultural events, and restaurants.

SUMMARY

Living, studying or *working* in another country can be difficult due to the many cultural and etiquette differences; however, the more you explore another's character the more comfortable you will feel. In addition, surprisingly, the differences seem to disappear or at least begin to feel natural.

TIME TO USE THE MATERIAL

1) Please fill in the blanks from this snippet of President Ronald Reagan's speech.

> "...the United States is the only country in the world that once you ____ in it, you can become a ____ of it. If you move to _____, you are never _____. If you move to _____, you are never a _____. But, when you move here, _____ can become an American."

2) What is a shared space?

_____

_____

3) What are the "Top Five Cultural Issues"?

_____

_____

_____

_____

_____

4) Is the "family name" used first or second when referring to someone?

_____

CHAPTER EIGHT
OFFICE POLITICS

POSITIVE OFFICE POLITICS

If you want to be effective and make your job easier, you will need to *interact* with those from all levels of the organization and they will need to interact with you. Therefore, the positive side of office politics could be that we all realize that the best way to get something from anyone is for that person to want to help you.

Nevertheless, *why* would anyone want to drop what he is doing to help you? Well, if you need a person's expert help, *you* need to be equally available when that person seeks assistance from you.

It is usually reciprocal; most often, you will receive what you give out. It is only human nature. Yet, if we use our position to attempt to *power over* others instead of remembering to treat others with respect, we will achieve – and receive – nothing.

Please consider this true story. One of my dearest friends is a manager in a professional-office setting. He has excellent manners and knows to treat others with respect. His office is next to his director's office, so he can hear when other managers stomp into the director's office demanding to see the director -- of course -- at that very moment. More often than not, they are turned away.

Alternately, my friend walks into the director's office, asks the director's assistant politely, using her name, and is typically offered an appointment that day.

Each of us needs to build trusted, helpful relationships with those below, at and above our level, so that in turn and in time they will assist us. These relationships require daily nurturing, always remembering to treat others as we wish to be treated. This is our *personal power*, a choice and knowledge of how to treat others.

NEGATIVE OFFICE POLITICS

THE POWER OF GOSSIP

Eventually, no matter where you work or position you hold you will be introduced to gossip, name-calling, and just plain negative office politics.

When you listen to those who gossip you are engaging in the activity. Therefore, inform the gossiper that you don't want to hear anything negative because you work with this person. Gossip breeds distrust. Do not allow the talk to spread.

When gossip is allowed to run rampant, people believe what they hear and soon the victim is eating her lunch alone and looking for another job. This was the case with one of my very best friends.

She was the newest employee in a typical office setting, while most of her fellow coworkers have been there for many years. Her job was to modify existing programs and to create new ones, which generated anxiety among her coworkers. Many are not comfortable with change, so soon the gossip began.

My friend is a strong young woman who realized what was happening. However, she was crushed when she received her evaluation saying that *she* cannot work well with others or alone. Taking a deep breath, she politely challenged the evaluation, and began looking for another job.

Who knows why these things happen. I relayed this story to another close friend – mentioning no names – to try to get some answers for myself. Even though she is twenty years older than my young friend, she shared a very similar story. The same thing happened to her in a law office twenty years ago. She left her position also. This is the power of gossip.

As you see this is a destructive force, which can and will cause good workers to leave. Businesses lose money every year in employee turnover. To train new employees for the same position repeatedly is costly.

BEWARE THE OFFICE ROMANCE

Office romance is another hazard. Furthermore, it most often fails. While many employers skirt the issue, most report being uncomfortable with it. Some agencies ask the parties to sign a 'Consensual Relationship Agreement' protecting the couple and the agency. If the romance fails, the less-senior employee would not be able to pursue litigation against the employer.

However, nothing protects the parties from the embarrassment of everyone knowing their personal life. Remember that when you are romantically involved you are also sharing your personal information. When the romance ends, your privacy may be compromised.

In addition, there always seems to be someone at fault for the breakup. The blame-game makes for a very uncomfortable situation, especially in the workplace. Therefore, it is best to date outside the workplace.

KEEP YOUR PRIVATE LIFE PRIVATE

Additionally, think twice before confiding personal information with your coworker. Office friendships frequently fail as well. Too often, we rush into relationships with our coworkers before realizing exactly who the person is. This could be a career-ending move as we find that we have told the office snoop how much we dislike our boss.

This brings up another absolute no-no: negative chatter about the company or superiors. It is morale oppressing and could be a career ender. You may find yourself scrambling to find a new job.

A great book about creating a positive workplace is, Fish, by Stephen C. Lundin Ph.D., Harry Paul, and John Christensen.

HOMEWORK

Examine your office politics. What can be improved? What can you do about making a change for the better?

TIME TO USE THE MATERIAL

1) What are the three "negative office politics" suggested in this chapter?

_____

_____

_____

CHAPTER NINE
NETIQUETTE

THE BASICS

In the workplace, email and the Internet is commonplace these days. However, many do not use their best manners or common sense. Our coworkers check their Facebook status during meetings, coworkers forward questionable jokes, and some even visit porn sites during their lunch break.

First, remember that every rule established for the workplace also refer to our email and online visits (including Social Networking sites).

Engaging in hate mongering – including all ethnicities, religions, ages, sexual orientation, cultures, and genders – in any fashion is an absolute no-no. Visiting sexually explicit sites are off limits. Spending valuable work time on-line for personal use is not appropriate, as would be excessive cellphone use. Moreover, avoid swearing, offensive language and harassment in emails.

"Just follow good old fashioned, proper behavior and you can't go wrong."
Charlotte Ford

Secondly, style is as important when composing email messages as it is with writing any business letter. Grammar, spelling, tone, and attention to the reader of the document are what we strive for in our business letters. Yet we send emails with letters standing for words (U for you), happy faces, and all capitals, which appear to the reader as if we are yelling. In addition, notes with acronyms like OYOT (on your own time) may be difficult for the reader to decode.

In addition, there is no body language in emails. Therefore, we should refrain from humor and sarcasm, which can be misunderstood. Note; typically, we do not use happy faces emojis in workplace emails—not professional. However, when emailing a colleague with whom you are on 'friendly' terms, it is common to relax these rules a bit. Workplace emojis are becoming more common in these cases.

Email is as permanent as any other written document we write. Just hitting the delete key does not guarantee it is removed from the depths of the hard drive. Anyone may read what you write. Once sent, it may be copied and circulated and it has your return address.

Never write anything in your email that you would not want posted on the bulletin board.

EMAIL IN THE WORKPLACE RULES

- Reread your messages before hitting send.
- Keep it short—shorter than hard-copy documents.
- Don't send an email for complicated issues; it's best to schedule a meeting instead.
- Do not forget the attachment.
- Do not use sarcastic humor, all caps, or acronyms.

- Use clear subject lines.

- Double check the recipient; don't send a message to the wrong person.

- Do not use anything that someone has written as your own or forward a message without permission.

- Do not forward jokes or political messages.

- Do not write when you're angry. It is called flaming.

- Check your email accounts often and reply promptly.

TELEPHONE ETIQUETTE

Typically, managers state their preferences for answering the telephone. However, stating your name and business using a pleasant tone of voice is standard.

Imagine correctly stating the preferred message while using a negative tone of voice. The caller may hang up and take his business elsewhere. Most importantly, always talk to the person on the phone as if he or she is present and in the same room with you.

Even when very busy and the calls are coming in rapidly, please refrain from answering the phone with: "Please hold." The person calling may only have a few minutes to talk and more than likely will not consider your request positively.

VOICE MAIL

When leaving a voice mail message, state your name slowly at the beginning and end of message, spelling it if necessary. Leave your number and get to the point.

When you receive a voice mail message, answer quickly. Check your voice mail often.

CELLPHONES

Do not use your cellphone while in another's presence. This includes texting. Thus, do not text while in meetings or in other's presence.

Be mindful about the ringing and volume of voice. Additionally, avoid excessive cellphone use, only using it on break

.

SOCIAL NETWORKING IN THE WORKPLACE

Social networking use in the workplace appears to be a normal part of most workers' day. However, just because it is commonplace doesn't mean that it is safe. It seems that there is a story every week about lost jobs and ruined relationships due to a lapse in judgment about a social media posting.

This has become such a problem that businesses have had to create a social networking/media policy. Most have common rules, such as not posting in the name of the business and not defaming the business or those with whom you work. Some may even have morality clauses, such as not posting racy images.

Nevertheless, no matter what rules are or are not in place, all of us should pause before posting. Reflect how the words or images may be viewed by others before hitting enter.

RULES

- No cyber dumping
- Beware of sharing personal information
- Do not post racy or potentially embarrassing photos
- Do not post hateful or untruthful gossip about others
- Do not use profanities or poor grammar
- Do not post as if you are representing your employer

- Do not discuss your job or employer on line
- Avoid discussing politics or religion

HOMEWORK

What do you post on social networking sites? Scrutinize your posts.

TIME TO USE THE MATERIAL

1) What are three of the bulleted "Email in the Workplace Rules"?

   _____

   _____

   _____

2) What are three of the six "Social Networking" rules?

   _____

   _____

   _____

CHAPTER TEN
BUSINESS MEETING ETIQUETTE

Business Meeting Basics

"Sleep not when others speak, Sit not when others stand, Speak not when you should hold your peace, Walk not on when others stop." George Washington

A successful business meeting begins with an early announcement, which allows all participants to have adequate time for maneuvering their schedules. Usually announced via email, it is especially successful if using the organization's shared drive.

The agenda should be open for all to read and to examine. This is the best way to ensure that no action item is assigned to a person who will not be present to negotiate it and that all are notified. Everyone should have an opportunity to read it and return comments well before the planned meeting.

Note

The weekly business meetings can be initiated by telephone or email, but written invitations are considered proper for all formal meetings.

The meeting room must be large enough for all, but not overly large to make attendees uncomfortable. It should be centrally located if possible. Everyone should be able to hear without an echo. Seating should be adequate, comfortable, and include tables to spread materials. Lighting should be adequate, without sun glare. Temperature should be on the cool side; the room will heat up with more bodies inhabiting it.

Recognition of others is always a necessity in every situation and is no less important for the business meeting. It is best to thank each participant verbally for his assistance and attendance. Follow-up with an email or a handwritten thank you card to those who were particularly helpful.

Typically, participants want to know if there was a reason for their participation. After all, they had to reschedule their day around the meeting. Minutes of the meeting can be very helpful in this endeavor. In these, the participants can read how their participation helped meet the stated objectives and about all the decisions that were made during the meeting.

HOMEWORK

List all the steps involved in creating a successful meeting.

FACILITATOR'S RESPONSIBILITIES

BASIC RULES

The facilitator of the business meeting has three very important duties to focus upon for a successful meeting. He/she needs to successfully facilitate participation, keep everyone on track, and must be able to handle a difficult person during the event.

If a subject is important enough to convene a meeting, be considerate of the participants' time and ensure that you are well prepared. Before the meeting, envision what type of meeting should be held. Consider how the participants will interact. Decide on the type of presentation to generate the most interest toward meeting the objectives. Always endeavor to create the proper atmosphere for promoting successful meetings.

The facilitator or most senior person schedules and calls the meeting. He communicates beforehand the objective of the meeting with a clear agenda with all items to be discussed, a clear beginning and ending time, and the location.

All participants should be informed about the meeting, confirm, and in agreement of items and time. The facilitator makes sure that everyone knows *why* the meeting is taking place and what is expected of each participant. For example, if someone is responsible for preparing a document for the meeting, it must be known.

She sets the ground rules on inappropriate behavior such as those arriving late, leaving early, side conversations, etc. It should be very clear to all what the rules are.

One manager I know decided to lock the meeting doors five minutes after the stated time of the meeting due to those who were continuously tardy. Being locked out changed that behavior quickly.

Time is very important in the workplace and each person's time should be respected. Therefore, of course, the chair would never be late. All meetings need to begin on time because some participants may have back-to-back meetings. Assigning a timekeeper may be the best solution for keeping the meeting on track and closing on time. Perhaps ask the timekeeper to announce the time at least ten minutes before the end of the meeting to give time for closure. In addition, only extend the meeting with everyone in agreement.

The facilitator is responsible for choosing the minute keeper. This person records the proceedings, decisions and action points and makes copies for everyone, including those absent from the meeting.

All materials should be available: notepads, writing tools, handouts, agenda, and nametags if there are a number of participants unknown to the group.

In addition, the facilitator would have all calls, except very important calls, intercepted. He also asks participants to turn off their cellphones.

He is also responsible for these special considerations. He introduces anyone who is not known to others, ensures that anyone with disabilities has access to the meeting and the tools to interact, and announces if the meeting is being recorded.

The facilitator also schedules appropriate breaks in long meetings. Meetings 90 minutes and over require a break. State when the meeting will resume.

There seems to be that one person who wants to talk about the broken copier or will create a circular disagreement during every meeting. A good facilitator will redirect the meeting back to the action items and will ensure the meeting stays on track. The best method seems to be to address this person directly saying that the issue is important and the two of you can discuss this privately, but the floor belongs to the current action item.

If an outside speaker is presenting, ensure that this person has everything that is required, such as a podium, microphone, A/V equipment, projector and screen. The speaker should also be advised of the layout of the building and any parking issues well before the scheduled meeting.

Include time in the schedule for summing up what has been accomplished and for clarifying assignments and responsibilities. Discuss deadlines for assigned tasks, future meeting dates, and questions (perhaps for future-meeting agenda items). Everyone should have an opportunity at the end of the meeting to have the floor for FYI items: future vacations, potential problems, etc. In addition, everyone should be thanked for his or her participation.

Send written notes of the meeting to all participants and those absent.

FORMAL MEETINGS

This type of business meeting can be a departmental meeting, board meeting, management meeting or negotiation, and usually has a set format, such as the chair or facilitator may be the same person each time.

All the paperwork (agendas, minutes, reports, etc.) is usually circulated well ahead of time for each participant to familiarize himself with the information.

All reports, which may include vital information such as statistics, should be issued at least three days before the meeting for all participants to peruse. Study each component of the meeting to be fully prepared. Dress appropriately and appear professional.

As with all business meetings, the facilitator should have all calls, except the utmost important calls, intercepted. Ask that all cellphones be turned off. Once again, a good facilitator will redirect the meeting back to the action items and will ensure the meeting stays on track.

Don't

- Schedule meetings on Fridays.

HOMEWORK

Imaging that you are the facilitator of a business meeting. How would you deal with an employee's continued tardiness?

PARTICIPANT'S RESPONSIBILITIES

RULES FOR ALL MEETINGS

Begin by replying to all invitations even if you cannot attend. If you can't attend, state why. Study the agenda to prepare for interaction. Ask if you are required to present any materials.

Be punctual and dress well. If you know that you will be late or you have back-to-back meetings, which may delay you, notify the organizer of the meeting as soon as you learn of this.

Turn off your cellphone. If just one phone rings during the meeting, the focus has changed from the action item to the offending phone. Pay attention to the task and try to forget about everything else.

Acknowledge any introductions or opening remarks with body language or verbally when appropriate. In addition, watch your body language. In a conference room, body language is 90% of the content.

Additionally, eat something so your stomach does not growl. Sit where you are directed to sit and ask if there is an established seating pattern.

During a formal meeting, if *you* are expected to participate with data, all reports, which may include vital information such as statistics that participants are *expected* to know, should be distributed at least three days before the meeting for all participants to peruse. However, if delivering a report or proposal do not hand these out until the end of the session. Participants will jump ahead to the conclusion and not listen.

Do Not

- Eat or drink unless the agenda states that it is appropriate.
- Use a cellphone.
- Text.
- Use a laptop, unless it has been requested.
- Chew gum or play with your pen.
- Arrive too early.

WHEN TO TALK

There is a definite pecking order. The more senior participants contribute before the lesser during discussions.

How to Talk

Always address the facilitator unless it is an open forum. Never interrupt anyone, even if you disagree strongly. You may return to it later with the facilitator's permission. Speak briefly and keep all comments relevant. When you state your opinion, don't ramble. Let the statement sit in a moment of silence. That opens the door to reaction and further dialogue

How To Disagree Politely

Do not use this forum to point out someone's mistakes or to take revenge for a slight. Some disagreements do not belong in a conference room. It may be best for two individuals to meet separately to address their differences.

If you are stating a difference of opinion, preface by stating your reasons for your position. It may even help to say you are just playing devil's advocate. Always address the problem, not the individual. Moreover, express your willingness to hear other opinions.

Just as the Vegas commercials state, "What happens here stays here." Everything that happens during the meeting is confidential unless agreed upon otherwise.

Homework

Imagine that you are responsible for presenting data during a formal meeting. What steps will you take for a successful meeting?

IF YOU ARE THE SPEAKER

PREPARE & DELIVER

If asked to give a presentation or speech, prepare. This would entail doing as much research as possible, having all handouts ready well before the meeting, and practice until you feel you are ready. Have a brief outline of your presentation available for the participants.

TIPS

- Research the attendees, expected number, interests, the type of organization, and location.
- Make local references; perhaps grab their attention with an appropriate quote or joke.
- Confirm that your needs are met concerning equipment.

- Plan well. Timing must be perfect and be respectful of the agenda.

- Arrive early to set up and mingle.

Personally, I have acted as presenter hundreds of times. As such, these tips come from experience and work well when followed, especially when presenting a difficult subject that attendees may not want to hear.

As with everything, we use proper manners and treat others as we wish to be treated with courtesy, kindness, and consideration.

HOMEWORK

Imagine that you are a guest speaker for an important meeting. How will you grab participant's attention at the beginning of your presentation?

Special Considerations

Electronic Meetings

Teleconferences and videoconferences – e-meetings – allow real time communication between principals in multiple locations and for decision making to be accomplished quicker. Money can also be saved in travel costs and time by conferencing.

Consider the special considerations for this type of meeting. Remember time zones. Scheduling a meeting for 10 am in California may be perfect for everyone in California. Nevertheless, there is a one-hour difference between California and Arizona.

Confirmations are crucial. Confirm participant's availability. Send all materials, including the agenda early for participants to peruse before the meeting. Confirm the arrival of materials. Confirm the availability of the technology you are using and ensure its reliability. It is embarrassing to begin your meeting only to find that the phone line is not working.

Finally, have all the phone numbers of participants ready and an extra phone line available just in case a line goes dead.

Stick to the agenda. Moreover, do not use graphs not included in the packets sent to each participants. It will not be seen in their screen.

If videoconferencing, consider the setting. What is behind you? The background of the room will be seen on participant's screens.

FAUX PAS

- Forgetting to mute the phone during a conference call.
- Tapping or making noise. Telephones will relay tapping, muted whispers, paper rustling and other distractions.
- Answering emails.
- Not identifying yourself. The other participants need to know who is talking.

COMMON NON-VERBAL & VERBAL MISTAKES

- Saying um or ah
- Humming or whistling
- Speaking too softly
- Using slang or profanity
- Using a first name without permission

- Chewing gum

Videoconferencing:
- Twiddling thumbs
- Tapping a foot or pencil
- Fidgeting
- Touching face or mouth
- Scratching your head
- Picking… anything
- Cleaning finger nails

BRAINSTORMING SESSIONS

Brainstorming sessions can be highly effective in gathering new ideas and creating an atmosphere where everyone feels as if he contributes.

Please consider everyone's contribution and do not dismiss anyone's ideas. Someone's crazy, offbeat idea just may be fine-tuned by the group to be the next 'big' thing.

Moreover, do not talk over anyone. Jot ideas down for discussion during a lull.

MEETING WITH CLIENTS

When meeting with clients schedule a room if you do not have an appropriate office space and close the door. Offer to care for the client's coat and offer her a seat.

Ensure that all materials are ready for the client and have them available. Have all participants in the meeting room waiting for the client if the meeting requires them. Introduce everyone at the beginning of the meeting.

Do not allow the phone to ring and turn off all cellphones. Offer your client coffee, tea, or some sort of beverage if the meeting lasts more than 30 minutes. Use real coffee mugs or cups--much better than paper.

If the client arrives too early, ask the receptionist to offer coffee or water and make the person feel comfortable. If there is no receptionist, come out to meet the client and offer coffee, water and something to read while waiting.

If the client is too late for a successful meeting, accept the reason and offer to reschedule. Always walk the client out to the reception area. If meeting with a client outside the office choose a neutral location so business and phones do not distract her.

IF FOOD AND DRINK WILL BE SERVED

First, ask yourself how much you need. It is best to offer caffeine and caffeine-free beverages. Some must refrain from caffeine and we should respect this. Serve neat to eat finger foods such as bagels instead of sticky buns.

If this is a catered lunch meeting and the clients will order food, limit selections. If lunch will be catered, ask about dietary concerns beforehand.

HOMEWORK

Imagine that you are responsible for organizing a lunch meeting at a nearby restaurant for your boss, your best client and you. What is your plan?

THE SIGNIFICANCE OF SEATING PATTERNS

Traditionally, the head of the table (the end farthest from the door) has been reserved for the leader of the meeting, with opposite seats for others of importance such as guests, senior management, or visitors.

Today, most often, the "power seat" is the middle of the table, with his or her staff on either side of that center seat, facing the door. Those he or she is meeting would sit on the opposite side of the table seated similarly.

However, during negotiations having the two sides on opposite sides of the table could set an adversarial tone to the meeting. So, to build a long-term relationship, consider sitting next to a person from the other side.

Final Notes

For Participants

Some disagreements do not belong in a conference room. If you are stating a difference of opinion, preface by stating your reasons for your position. Always address the problem, not the individual.

- Express your willingness to hear other opinions.
- Body language is 90% of the content.
- Short stories that help support a point are useful.

Do Not

- Ramble when you state your opinion.
- Try to mask grogginess by holding your head in your hands (bad body language!).
- Get angry.

- Dominate the meeting.

- Be afraid of adding humor (particularly self-deprecating) to your statements.

FOR FACILITATORS

Invite those who will participate. Create and forward an agenda.

Assign a timekeeper and scribe. Set ground rules on inappropriate behavior about arriving late, leaving early, and side conversations.

Some disagreements do not belong in a conference room. It may be best for the two individuals to meet separately to address their differences.

If you are stating a difference of opinion, preface by stating your reasons for your position. It may even help to say you are just playing devil's advocate.

When you state your opinion, do not ramble. Let the statement sit in a moment of silence. Open the door to reaction and further dialogue. Always address the problem, not the individual.

Express your willingness to hear other opinions.

Watch your body language. In a conference room, body language is 90% of the content

Make sure you know the role of each person in the room. Practice your recall of names. Write down the names of everyone in the room in the order of their seating position. Say the person's name when speaking to him as a sign of respect and openness

Short stories that help support a point can make a huge difference.

If you are feeling groggy, do not try to mask it by holding your head in your hands (bad body language!). Just get up and get a cup of coffee or refreshment if there is some in the room. You might even suggest the entire group take a short break.

Use your time between meetings to network with others. Trust is much stronger with those you get to know personally.

If you are in a negotiation, do not be afraid to mix up the seating order. Having the two sides on opposite sides of the table sets an adversarial tone. If you are trying to build a long-term relationship, sit next to a person from the other side. Sitting in the middle of the table creates a more open atmosphere of collegiality.

Establish clear assignments and deadlines at the end of the meeting.

Do Not

- Have a meeting if you do not need one.
- Get angry. It does not help matters, and will shut down the conversation faster than an earthquake.
- Dominate the meeting.
- Be afraid of adding humor (particularly, self-deprecating humor) to your statements.

- Be afraid of clichés (e.g. "not enough horses pulling this wagon", or "that dog don't hunt").

TIME TO USE THE MATERIAL

1) How do we begin a successful business meeting?

_____

_____

2) What are the six elements required to ensure attendees are comfortable in the meeting?

_____

_____

_____

_____

_____

_____

3) What the "three important duties" a facilitator should focus upon for a successful meeting?

_____

_____

_____

4) What are the five tips all presenters should use?

_____

_____

_____

_____

5) What are three of the eight common videoconferencing non-verbal and verbal mistakes?

_____

_____

_____

CHAPTER ELEVEN
BUSINESS MEAL ETIQUETTE

KNOW BEFORE YOU GO!

SOCIAL MANNERS VS BUSINESS MANNERS

"Good manners will open doors that the best education cannot." Clarence Thomas

The manners we use in social situations are different from those we use in business situations. This is important to note for all business encounters. For example, men open doors for women socially; yet in the business world, we open doors for everyone.

In the past, a man was introduced *to* a woman when in social situations—not so in business. Rank is more significant in business. Thus, we always introduce people to the higher-ranking person first: "Mr. or Ms. Higher Ranked, I would like to introduce *to you* Mr. or Ms. Lesser Rank. Gender is not an issue.

Subsequently, when introducing your manager to a new employee, say the manager's name first and then the new employee. For example, "Ms. Gutierrez, I would like to introduce to you, our newest employee, Ralph Brown."

A client is considered most important or the highest rank. Say the client's name first and then your manager's name if you are introducing your client to your manager. For example, "Ms. Applegate, I would like to introduce to you, our manager, Ms. Gutierrez."

In social situations, people may or may not extend their hands signaling a wish to shake hands. In business, everyone shakes hands, although we typically wait for the most senior people to extend his/her hand first. We grip the other person's hand with equal pressure using a dry right hand.

If seated while being introduced, stand. Smile and shake hands firmly, while maintaining good eye contact. Repeat the other person's name and greet him or her with, "It is so nice to meet you."

GENDER ETIQUETTE

In business, there is no gender preference. Treating a woman as we would in a social setting could be viewed as gratuitous and demeaning.

HOMEWORK

Are there other social manners different from business manners you can mention?

RESTAURANT MEALS

Table manners are essential so don't leave them at home.

The meal may appear to be just a meal; however, potential clients or employers may be scrutinizing your meal behavior and manners, which could be an indication of future problems.

A dear friend shared a story with me about a dinner he had attended with his coworkers and boss. Usually during these typically pleasant dinners, many tasks were accomplished. However, this particular dinner included a new employee who surprised the group with his atrocious table manners making everyone uncomfortable. As a result, not much was accomplished that evening and he was dismissed the next day. Message: don't be that guy!

If you are the first to arrive for a business meal at a restaurant, choose a chair at the center of the table, unless you are the highest ranking, a special client or guest. Actually, my first choice is to wait for the others to arrive. This is the best way to ensure that you do not step on anyone's shoes—or sit in his chosen seat.

First impressions are imperative and meals may be the first time business associates meet you. So focus on your body language. Sit tall, not too stiffly and do not rock or tip back in your chair. Do not comb your hair, pick at your teeth, or apply makeup, even if you are alone at the table at the time.

Wait for everyone to arrive and seated before placing your napkin in your lap. Most likely, you will stand to shake hands and your napkin could fall to the floor. In addition, you may appear too eager to eat.

Good conversational skills are critical; business is rarely the only topic discussed. Become well rounded by studying current news and cultural events. Humor is welcome at the table but ethnic or questionable jokes are not. Do not dominate the conversation, allow others their input, and remember that we share at the table. Keep the conversation light and friendly and watch your language.

When it is time to order, listen to what the host is ordering and try to order something similar if being treated. It wouldn't be appropriate to order a full meal only to find that everyone else is ordering a small salad.

If this is an interview meal, listen to what is being ordered and *again* order similarly. Do not order any item that could splatter on your clothes like pasta in a light broth. You wouldn't want anything that could distract you from the interview. Avoid foods that would get your hands messy; for example, shrimp in the shell.

Great example of a dish to avoid!

Chicken breasts or fish with vegetables is usually a perfect choice because they are easy to cut and eat. Salads are a good choice too if you cut the vegetables into small bites and are careful about the dressing. Perhaps ask for the dressing to be presented on the side. Avoid alcohol even if everyone else is imbibing. You can celebrate later if you get the job.

Take your Table Manners

Now is the real test of your skills. The food has arrived and your napkin is in your lap. Which utensil do you use? Choose the outermost fork or spoon. Use the fork to stab or scoop solid food items. Alternately, to scoop a liquid, use the spoon.

Hold your fork in your non-dominant hand (usually left) tines down, index finger along the spine. While holding the food with the fork, cut one bite at a time with the knife in the palm of your right hand and your index finger guiding it. Place the knife on the edge of the plate, sharp edge toward you and transfer the fork to your right hand to pick up the bite.

Eat soup by picking up the larger spoon (on the far right) and hold it similarly to a pencil. Scoop the soup away from you.

This method is referred to as the American Method and is widely used in the United States. Although there is another method that we will not discuss here, the point is that we hold our utensils correctly and not as a shovel.

There are a few absolute *don't (s)* we should discuss. We never eat with our elbows sticking out as if we are flying and never return a used utensil to the table. Instead, place it on the edge of the plate, and we eat only one bite at a time. The table manners our elders taught us years ago are still in vogue; please use them.

Also, say please and thank you when appropriate. Say excuse me when temporarily leaving the table or when coughing and sneezing. These magic words work as well now as when we were children. If you have a cough or sneeze attack, excuse yourself from the table until your spell in under control.

Never use your napkin to blow your nose; use it only to blot your mouth. Moreover, do so before drinking if you have recently taken a bite. It is unsightly to have food or grease on the lip of a glass.

Eat with your mouth closed and don't talk until you have finished the bite. Do not hover over your food; instead lean forward slightly to take a bite. While taking a bite, do not use your finger to guide the food onto your fork.

When bread is on the table, it is fine to help yourself once the entrée has arrived. Never reach over a tablemate. Rather, ask for the bread to be passed. Place the bread on the bread plate (yours would be above your forks) or your entree plate. If you use butter, place this on your plate. Tear a small piece of bread, butter it, and eat one piece at a time. Try not to take the last piece of bread if tablemates have not chosen a piece.

Be kind to those around you. Remember to include all in the conversation and smile. Also, remember to be kind to the wait staff. When you are kind to everyone at the table and then treat the wait staff as though they are below you, you are exhibiting a disturbing contrast. You may be perceived as a person who treats others kindly in order to further your own agenda. In essence, this behavior creates distrust.

At the end of the meal, thank the host if you have been treated. If not, you should have calculated your portion as you ordered. Leave the appropriate amount including a twenty percent tip. Do not make everyone wait as you are trying to figure out your total. If you are the host, pay the bill as quickly as possible to avoid any awkwardness. Now place your napkin on the right side of the plate and thank everyone for the fine discussion.

As you may have noticed, the etiquette we use for business meals is no different from any other situation.

Note

- Always use your best behavior and turn your cellphone off!

- Dress appropriate for the occasion.

- A business meal is never about the food.

- Take a cough or sneeze attack away from the table.

- Blow your nose away from the table.

- Blot your mouth before taking a drink.

- Don't push food onto your fork with your finger.

- Don't discuss business before the first course has arrived.

- Watch your host for table manners clues.

- Do not offer your business card unless someone asks for it.

HOMEWORK

Practice your skills! Write a thank you note to one who purchased your meal.

Buffet & Cocktail Receptions

"There is no accomplishment so easy to acquire as politeness, and none so profitable."George Bernard Shaw

Many times a business meal could be buffet style with a number of people with whom you are expected to mingle, which can be very stressful to the mingling skills disadvantaged. A cocktail reception is another potential minefield. Here we will discuss these two situations. The suggestions are the same for both.

First, you may be faced with the ubiquitous nametag. Most people place it on their left shoulder, which seems appropriate because most are right-handed, and this seems the easiest to maneuver. However, the correct position is on your right shoulder.

There is an excellent reason for this. We shake hands with our right hand. The person shaking your hand will first glance at your face, your nametag (because it is in his eye-line), and finally your hand. He will then glance at your nametag again when he finishes shaking your hand. This is great face/name recognition in your favor.

It is best not to arrive hungry. Remember, this event is more about mingling and networking than eating. Yet, you will most probably want to sample the buffet. Please do this as soon as you arrive.

It is best if plates and forks will be available, but it isn't always the case. If so, try to choose items that you can eat with one bite using your fork. If there are no forks or plates, use a napkin and toothpicks. Arrange no more than two items on your napkin and eat those with your toothpick.

Please do not stand at the buffet table and eat. Walk away and come back for a couple more items. However, please do not spend much more than 10-15 minutes eating.

Because you will always want a clean, dry hand to shake the hand of others, eat and drink at separate times. When finished eating, find a non-alcohol beverage to enjoy while strolling around the room.

Please keep your glass in your left hand to keep your right hand dry.

Mingling is a focal point of these events. Therefore, it is important to brush up on your mingling skills. Approach those whose body language seems to signal openness and introduce yourself. Most importantly, treat everyone as though that person is special.

The purpose of small talk is to find something in common and create a bond. This is best accomplished by listening, being observant, and asking pertinent questions. *Listen more than talk.*

Honor everyone's personal space and disposition. Avoid intense conversations and weighty discussions, such as marriage, politics, or religion. Maintain good eye contact and watch your body language.

CONVERSATION TOPICS

Before the affair, think of at least three topics. Spend 5-10 minutes talking to one person and move on. If possible, learn something about the guests so you are better prepared to ask pertinent questions. Avoid excess giggling, throat clearing or keeping your hands in your pockets.

- *Good:* Current events, work, books, sports
- *Not:* Religion, sex, politics, illness, cursing or gossip

EATING AND DRINKING

- Use a napkin if you are carrying food.

- Eat quickly and do not hold court at the buffet table.

- Do not eat and drink at the same time.

- Try to arrange food on your plate in a way that it will be easy to eat in one bite.

- Use toothpicks if available.

- Keep drink in left hand; no alcohol.

Networking & Mingling Skills

Dress Appropriately!

Business casual is usually acceptable, but including a jacket is best. If the event is a fundraiser, wear formalwear. If in doubt, call.

Avoid wearing jewelry on the right hand or wrist. You will be shaking hand with many attendees and the jewelry will be in the way.

No visible tech objects, like cellphones and Bluetooth devices. Turn the cellphone off!

What is Networking & why do we do it?

Networking is a business/social event that is not business as usual and definitely not social. The rules, so clear to us during the business day, become a blur.

Networking is an activity designed to make connections that may help you in your career or business. It is a time to show off the best of you. But, be careful! You will be judged within the first 30 seconds. So, watch your body language, posture and walk with purpose. Work the room well.

Create an Elevator Speech

Create a one-minute commercial to introduce yourself. The goal is to connect your background to the organization's need or to create interest. Practice it until you know it well.

BEFORE THE AFFAIR

Do your homework. Find out who will be attending the event. Know your audience so you can ask pertinent questions. Visit attendee's websites if possible so you will have at least three topics to discuss.

BUSINESS CARD

A business card is an extension of who you are. Therefore, carry a card wallet to keep your cards in pristine condition. Accept another's card as if it is special; read it and put it away.

Bring plenty of cards, but wait until it seems appropriate to give it to someone.

Try to take notes about those you meet on their business card. Enter the information you've gathered onto a spread sheet.

FOLLOW-UP IS EVERYTHING

- Email, call, and send thank you notes.

COMMON FINGER FOODS

This section – and the next – is simply for your information only. You would never use your hands to eat many of these foods during a business meal. In fact, you would never order most of them. However, this information along with the next section is valuable.

- Artichoke
- Asparagus
- Bacon, if it is crisp
- Sandwiches
- Cookies
- Small fruit or berries with stems
- French fries and potato chips
- Hamburgers and hot dogs
- Corn on the cob
- Caviar
- Pickles
- Olives
- Tacos

How Do I Eat These?

Apples:

Quarter apples with a fruit knife or steak knife; the core is cut away from each piece and pieces are eaten with the fingers. If you choose to remove the skin, pare each piece separately.

Artichoke:

Eat artichokes with the fingers one leaf at a time. Dip leaves into the sauce provided. Eat the fleshy part of the leaf, scraping it off between your teeth. Place the leaf on the side of your plate. Remove the choke, the small leaves with sharp points, with your spoon and add to the eaten leaves. Cut the heart into sections using a fork and knife, and dip with the fork into the sauce to eat.

Asparagus:

At a formal dinner, use a fork and knife, cutting one bite at a time. Individual tongs may be used at a *very* formal dinner. In casual settings, asparagus is a finger food if firm and not in a sauce.

Bananas:

At a *formal meal*, peel the banana with fork and knife, eating one bite at a time. However, a whole banana would not be served at a formal meal. Thus, you would eat each smaller piece with a fork and knife. For informal meals, use your hands.

Barbecued Meats:

Barbeque is informal. Hot dogs, hamburgers, ribs and small chicken pieces are treated as finger food. To eat steak, fish, and large chicken pieces, use a fork and steak knife, cutting one bite at a time. Add sauce to your plate, if desired.

Berries:

In a formal setting, a strawberry fork may be used—just spear. If they have a stem, it is finger food. Ladle the sauce or cream onto your fruit plate before dipping.

Bread and Butter:

Break off a small piece of bread, place butter onto the bread plate using a butter knife. Use your knife to spread butter onto bread.

Caviar:

Caviar is finger food. Use the caviar spoon, usually small and round, and place a small amount on your plate or triangular toast that is usually served with caviar. If condiments are served, such as chopped onion, place a small amount on top of the caviar.

Cheese:

Spread soft cheeses such as Brie with the knife provided onto crackers or bread. With firmer cheeses, use the knife to slice a piece and place it onto your plate.

Cherry Tomatoes:

Cherry tomatoes are finger foods, unless it is served in a salad or other entrée. Break the skin in your mouth before chewing. If they are served in a salad or other dish, cut and eat using the fork. Prick the skin to allow the juice to run first to avoid a messy juice explosion.

Chicken:

Never eat chicken with the fingers in a formal dining situation. In an informal setting, you can eat the smaller pieces with the fingers unless it is in a sauce. Larger pieces, such as chicken breasts must be cut using a place or steak knife.

Clams and Oysters:

While holding the shell in one hand and fork in the other, spear the clam, dip it in the sauce and eat it in one bite. You may suck the clam or oyster off the shell at an informal setting.

Condiments:

Place the condiments on to your plate before adding to a food item.

Corn on the Cob:

This is an informal food and is never served at a formal event. Eat with your fingers.

Crackers for Soup:

Place crackers for soup onto the bread plate. Break up into pieces and scatter into the soup.

Grapes:

Snap off a cluster, place on your plate and eat one at a time with fingers.

Lobster:

Pull the meat out with cocktail fork and dip it into melted butter or any sauce that is provided. Eat the tail meat by pulling out one piece at a time. If you pull out a particularly large piece, cut it with your dinner knife or fork before dipping.

Place the empty shell pieces onto a separate waste bowl or plate.

Melon:

At informal meals, melon is considered a finger food; however, it should be eaten with a fork and knife at other times.

Mussels:

Spear mussel, dip in sauce and eat it.

Oranges or Another Citrus:

In formal meals, cut off top and bottom, and slice off peel. Eat segments with fingers or fork and knife. For informal meals, peel with your hands.

Papaya:

Cut papaya in half; take out seeds with spoon, placing seeds on the side of plate. Eat with a fork or spoon.

Peas:

Scoop onto your fork or push using bread or your knife. Never guide with your finger.

Pizza:

Eat with a fork and knife unless the slices are firm.

Salad:

It is always best to use both a fork and knife.

Shish Kabob:

Hold the shish kabob in one hand and use the dinner fork to remove the pieces with the other. Place the stick on the side of the plate. Eat with a fork and knife.

Shrimp:

Small shrimp may be dipped into cocktail sauce using the cocktail fork. Eat large shrimp with fork and knife and place sauce on plate.

Snails/Escargot:

Pick up one at a time using tongs and remove with a cocktail fork—dip into butter.

Soups:

Eat clear soup with a small, round spoon, never filling more than 75% full. Eat from the side of the spoon, never placing the entire spoon into your mouth.

A cream soup is served with a medium round spoon, chunky soups with a large round spoon, and an oval spoon is used for all types of soup and some desserts.

A cup with handle may be picked up and drunk. Never pick up a bowl to drink the soup and never slurp. Place the spoon on the side of the plate when finished.

Spaghetti:

Never cut pasta with fork and knife. Use a fork and twirl until the strands are firmly wrapped around the fork. If there are strands dangling from the fork, take the bite allowing the strands to fall to the plate, use the fork to guide the strands.

Sushi:

Sushi may be eaten with the fingers or chopsticks.

TIME TO USE THE MATERIAL

1) What are the differences between social and business manners?

_____

_____

_____

_____

2) What is my suggestion of a perfect business meal choice?

_____

_____

3) Name three bulleted "Notes" from the Take Your Table Manners section.

_____

_____

_____

4) Name three bulleted rules concerning buffets.

_____

_____

_____

CHAPTER TWELVE: ANSWERS TO QUIZ QUESTIONS

YOUR ANSWERS

CHAPTER ONE

1) Why is etiquette in the workplace important?

- We are better able to create the type of working environment in which we wish to work.

2) Why is projecting a positive attitude important in the workplace?

- Your attitude is how others perceive you.
- Additionally, displaying a positive attitude aids in creating a positive work environment.

CHAPTER TWO

1) What is the most important component of communication?

- Listening, attentive listening is best.

2) Why is constructive feedback so important?

- Positive constructive feedback helps all of us to improve ourselves.

CHAPTER THREE

1) What percentage of what we see do we remember?

Fill in the blanks:

Honesty is <u>imperative</u> in the <u>workplace</u>; in fact, it is imperative in <u>everything</u> we do.

CHAPTER FOUR

1) Why is body language so important in the workplace?

- Our body language displays to others how we feel about ourselves. People believe what they see. So, if we want to be viewed as professional, we need to display excellent body language and posture.

2) Why is attire choice so important?

- Others will judge us either profession or not partly by our clothing choices.

3) Studies support the fact that observers trust and believe those who *appear* more successful, educated and capable. What is one of those elements that helps us "appear" more successful?

- Color and quality of the material of our clothing.

4) What is the basic definition of "Corporate Attire"?

- This dress code applies to law firms, investment banking, and any company that is considered conservative

CHAPTER FIVE

1) What are the tools for working with the deaf?

- Do not shout.
- Get the person's attention and speak clearly.
- Notes help; email and texting are great tools as well.

2) What behavior is best when talking to a person in a wheelchair?

- When talking to those in wheelchairs, sit in a chair if possible to establish eye contact.

CHAPTER SIX

1) What is the best strategy to use with angry customers?

- Place yourself in his shoes. Step back, lower your voice and speak softly, repeating what you believe the problem is. Then, seek help if you can't solve the issue.
- Never say that it isn't your job.

CHAPTER SEVEN

1) Please fill in the blanks from this snippet of President Ronald Reagan's speech.

"...the United States is the only country in the world that once you <u>live</u> in it, you can become a <u>part</u> of it. If you move to <u>France</u>, you are never a <u>Frenchman</u>. If you move to <u>Germany,</u> you are never a <u>German</u>. But, when you move here, <u>anyone</u> can become an American."

2) What is a "Shared Space"?

Shared Space" is the term I use to describe places the public shares, like the workplace, stores, restaurants, etc.

3) What are the "Top Five Cultural Issues"?

- How women are viewed

- Personal freedoms

- Individualism

- Time

- Discussing work

4) Is the "family name" used first or second when referring to someone?

- Second

CHAPTER EIGHT

1) What are the three "negative office politics" mentioned in this chapter?

- Gossip

- The office romance

- Sharing too much personal information

CHAPTER NINE

1) What are three of the bulleted "Email in the Workplace Rules"? All eleven are:

- Reread your messages before hitting send.

- Keep it short—shorter than hard-copy documents.

- Don't send an email for complicated issues; it's best to schedule a meeting instead.

- Do not forget the attachment.

- Do not use sarcastic humor, all caps, or acronyms.

- Use clear subject lines.

- Double check the recipient; don't send a message to the wrong person.

- Do not use anything that someone has written as your own or forward a message without permission.

- Do not forward jokes or political messages.

- Do not write when you're angry. It is called flaming.

- Check your email accounts often and reply promptly.

2) What are three of the six "social networking" rules?

All six are:

- No cyber dumping

- Beware of sharing personal information

- Do not post racy or potentially embarrassing photos

- Do not post hateful or untruthful gossip about others

- Do not use profanities or poor grammar

- Do not post as if you are representing your employer

CHAPTER TEN

1) How do we begin a successful business meeting?

- We begin a successful business meeting with an early announcement, typically via email.

2) What are the six elements required to ensure attendees are comfortable in the meeting?

- Room must be large enough for all, but not overly large.

- Room should be centrally located.

- Everyone should be able hear without an echo.

- Seating should be adequate, comfortable, and include tables to spread materials.

- Lighting should be adequate, without sun glare.

- Temperature should be on the cool side; the room will heat up with more bodies inhabiting it.

3) What the "three important duties" a facilitator should focus upon for a successful meeting?

- Successfully facilitate participation

- Keep everyone on track

- Must be able to handle a difficult person during the event

4) What are the five tips all presenters should use?

- Research the attendees, expected number, interests, the type of organization, and location.

- Make local references; perhaps grab their attention with an appropriate quote or joke.

- Confirm that your needs are met concerning equipment.

- Plan well. Timing must be perfect and be respectful of the agenda.

- Arrive early to set up and mingle.

5) What are three of the eight common videoconferencing non-verbal and verbal mistakes?

All eight are:

- Twiddling thumbs
- Tapping a foot or pencil
- Fidgeting
- Touching face or mouth
- Scratching your head
- Picking…anything
- Cleaning finger nails

CHAPTER ELEVEN

1) What are the differences between social and business manners?

- Women are, typically, treated differently, as rank is more important than gender in business.
- Socially, we may or may not shake hands. However, in business, everyone shakes hands.

2) What is my suggestion of a perfect business meal choice?

- Chicken breasts or fish with vegetables

3) Name three bulleted "Notes" from the Take Your Table Manners section.

All rules are:

- Always use your best behavior and turn your cellphone off!

- Dress appropriate for the occasion.

- A business meal is never about the food.

- Take a cough or sneeze attack away from the table.

- Blow your nose away from the table.

- Blot your mouth before taking a drink.

- Don't push food onto your fork with your finger.

- Don't discuss business before the first course has arrived.

- Watch your host for table manners clues.

- Do not offer your business card unless someone asks for it.

4) Name three bulleted rules concerning buffets.

All rules are:

- Use a napkin if you are carrying food.

- Eat quickly and do not hold court at the buffet table.

- Do not eat and drink at the same time.

- Try to arrange food on your plate in a way that it will be easy to eat in one bite.

- Use toothpicks if available.

- Keep drink in left hand; no alcohol.

ABOUT YOUR AUTHOR

Your author, Rebecca Black, also known as The Polite One, recently retired from her company **Etiquette Now!** after a successful and rewarding 20+ years.   As the owner and facilitator of her company, this retired elementary school teacher designed and presented custom etiquette workshops for the individual, corporate, governmental and educational client.   Due to her extensive knowledge of the subject, she is also a well-respected author of etiquette books and lesson plans.

Considered an expert in the field, Rebecca answers etiquette questions (Q & A) and offers advice through her blogs: Got Etiquette Advice, Got Wedding Etiquette, and The Polite One's Insights.

Although for many years, Rebecca, focused her writing on etiquette issues, she is currently following her passion of writing fiction. A few of her most recent children's books also focus on the environment: *Save the Jellywonkers: Help Keep The Oceans Clean; Beware the Blackness, A Jellywonker Adventure;* and *The Tale of a Bear & Pony: A Yellowstone Adventure*

Please visit rebeccablackauthor.blogspot.com for more information about Rebecca's current news.

Connect with Us

https://www.facebook.com/ThePoliteOne

https://www.facebook.com/rebeccablackauthor/

Visit Us

Rebecca Black Author

Etiquette Now! Insights

Got Etiquette Advice

Got Wedding Etiquette

Living Well & Enjoying Life—Rebecca Style

The Polite One's Insights

The Polite Traveler

https://www.amazon.com/author/rebecca_black

Published Fiction Books by Rebecca Black

The Tale of a Bear & Pony; A Yellowstone Adventure

Save The Jellywonkers! -- Help Keep Our Oceans Clean

Beware the Blackness! A Jellywonker Adventure

Sapphire and the Atlantians

War in Atlantis

The Return of the Tui Suri

Published Etiquette Books by Rebecca Black

Dining Etiquette: Essential Guide for Table Manners, Business Meals, Sushi, Wine and Tea Etiquette

Dress for All Occasions—The Basics, Attire Must-Haves, Dress Code Definitions & FAQs

Entertaining Skills 101

Etiquette for the Important Events in Our Lives: Common sense etiquette with a side of history and a dollop of gift-giving savvy

Etiquette for the Socially Savvy Adult: Life Skills for All Situations

Etiquette for the Socially Savvy Teen: Life Skills for All Situations

Golf Etiquette: Civility on the Course

How to Tea: British Tea Times

How to Teach Your Children Manners: Essential Life Skills Your Child Needs to Know!

International Business Travel Etiquette: Seal the Deal by Understanding Proper Protocol

Reaching Your Potential: How to use our life lessons to grow as a person and to improve the workplace environment

Societal Rage: Problem solving for our increasingly violent world

Sushi Etiquette: The guide for those who wish to eat sushi properly and avoid insulting the chef

Train the Trainer Guide: The essential guide for those who wish to present workshops and classes for adults

Wedding & Reception Planning: The Etiquette Guide for Planning the Perfect Wedding

Wine Etiquette--From holding the glass to ordering a bottle of wine in a restaurant and everything in-between

Workplace Etiquette: How to Create a Civil Workplace

Published Lesson Plans

Business Meal Etiquette

Career Fair Etiquette

Entertaining Skills 101: Lesson Plans for Those Who Wish to Present Workshops

Etiquette for the Socially Savvy Teen

Golf Etiquette

Growing Up Socially Savvy

How to Become a Socially Savvy Lady

How to Tea; British Tea Times

How to Teach Your Children Manners

Just for Teens, Skills for the Socially Savvy

Manners for Children

Organizational Skills

Prom Etiquette

Proper Business Attire

Skills for the Socially Savvy and Well-Dressed Teen

Skills for the Socially Savvy and Well-Organized Teen

Table Manners

Train the Trainer

Wine Etiquette

Workplace Etiquette

Wedding Lesson Plans

Lessons for the Newly Engaged

Wedding Planning

Wedding Reception Planning

Please visit https://www.amazon.com/author/rebecca_black for information about collecting more etiquette books.

www.ingramcontent.com/pod-product-compliance
Lightning Source LLC
Chambersburg PA
CBHW071427180526
45170CB00001B/247